Waffen-SS
in Combat

Text by Robert Michulec
Edited by Tom Cockle
Color plates by Ronald Volstad

PUBLICATIONS COMPANY

We welcome authors who can help
expand our range of books. If you
would like to submit material,
please feel free to contact us.

We are always on the look-out for new,
unpublished photos for this series.
If you have photos or slides or
information you feel may be useful to
future volumes, please send them to us
for possible future publication.
Full photo credits will be given upon
publication.

ISBN 962-361-645-7
printed in Hong Kong

The Waffen-SS had its origins in the post WWI Nazi organization known as the SA - Sturmabteilung - the storm troops headed by Ernst Röhm. In the early 1920s, a small group of men within the SA were formed into Hitler's personal bodyguard, at first known as "Stosstruppe Adolf Hitler". They later became known as the Schutz Staffel - protection squad - or SS for short. By 1929, they numbered less than 300 men, as compared to more than a quarter million in the SA, and held no special place in the organization. However, that year Heinrich Himmler was given command of the SS and during the next five years, membership rose to 30,000. By this time, the strength of the SA had grown to more than 3 million, and Hitler had serious concerns about control of this large, private army controlled by Röhm.

On June 30, 1934, Röhm and his SA leaders were arrested and shot to prevent a supposed coup attempt, with the SS providing the firing squads, an event which came to be known as "The Night of the Long Knives".

In the following years, under Himmler's guidance, the SS took over political police work in Germany, working its way into many areas of the Nazi party and various functions of the government.

By 1939, there were two distinct and separate parts, the Allgemeine-SS or general SS, the political and bureaucratic arm, and the armed SS, the SS-Verfügungstruppe, known after 1940 as the Waffen-SS.

The first combat units of the SS-Verfügungstruppe were the Leibstandarte Adolf Hitler, SS-Standarte 1 "Deutschland", SS-Standarte 2 "Germania" and SS-Standarte 3 "Der Führer". They had been trained during the period 1937-1939 to combat readiness under the direction of SS-Gruppenführer Paul Hausser, a former Wehrmacht general.

In September 1939, "LAH", under SS-Obergruppenführer "Sepp" Dietrich, fought as a regiment under 10.Armee in Poland while "Germania" served under 14.Armee and "Deutschland" formed part of Panzer-Division "Kempf". "Der Führer" occupied defensive positions on the West Wall. In October, the three SS-Standarte were combined to create the first SS field division, officially called SS-VT Division (mot.), with Hausser in command. In addition, there were five regiments of Totenkopfsturmbanne, low quality units formed from security police and concentration camp guards under the command of SS-Gruppenführer Theodor Eicke.

Three regiments served on occupation duty in Poland. They were then pulled back to Germany and, along with other Totenkopf units, SS-VT and Allgemeine-SS units, formed into the SS-Totenkopf-Division.

Due to recruiting restrictions placed on the SS, Himmler was only able to expand his combat units by recruiting men as security personnel into his Totenkopf units and then transferring them into the combat units. In this manner, ten new Totenkopf regiments were raised in 1939-40.

The following spring, LAH and SS-Verfügungsdivision, as it was now called, made a good showing during the battle of France but the inferior SS-Totenkopf-Division suffered heavy casualties, their record further stained by the murder of 100 British prisoners at Le Paradis.

Another low quality unit created in 1939 from members of the Ordnungspolizei was the Polizei-Division, under SS command but not actually part of the Waffen-SS until February 1942. They served in occupation duties in Poland and saw some limited action in France in 1940 before being transferred to Russia just after the beginning of Operation Barbarossa.

In December 1940, Regiment "Nordland", Danish and Norwegian volunteers, and Regiment "Westland", made up of Dutch and Flemish volunteers, were combined with "Germania" from the SS-Verfügungsdivision to form SS-Division (mot.) "Germania". By the end of December, it had been renamed SS-Division "Wiking". Committed to the Eastern Front for the entire war, it earned a good reputation as a fighting unit.

In late 1940, 6. and 7.SS-Totenkopf-Standarte were transferred to Norway and combined to form SS-Kampfgruppe "Nord". It was upgraded to divisional status in early June 1941 and renamed SS-Division "Nord". It saw action with the Finnish Army but did not perform well against the battle hardened Soviet troops who had fought in the Russo-Finnish War. The division was again renamed SS-Gebirgs-Division "Nord" and then 6.SS-Gebirgs-Division "Nord".

The seventh Waffen-SS division to be established was the SS-Freiwilligen-Division "Prinz Eugen", established in March 1942 with ethnic Germans from the Balkan states with Austrian and Rumanian officers. They were used solely in anti-partisan actions in the Balkans thereby freeing desperately needed regular troops for the Russian

Front. Later renamed 7.SS-Freiwilligen-Gebirgs-Division "Prinz Eugen", many of their personnel were tried and executed after the war for atrocities.

8.SS-Kavallerie-Division "Florian Geyer" was originally formed in September 1939 as 1.SS-Totenkopf-Reiterstandarte and was stationed in Warsaw in May 1940. It was used mainly behind the front lines in security and anti-partisan duties and was also suspected of many atrocities. Originally commanded by SS-Standartenführer Hermann Fegelein, who later became Himmler's liaison officer to Hitler, it was destroyed in Budapest in 1945.

9.SS-Panzer-Division "Hohenstaufen" was created in December 1942 with young conscripts under the command of SS-Gruppenführer Wilhelm Bittrich, seeing action in Poland in the spring of 1944 and in France, mainly around Caen, during that summer. Retreating through France and Holland, they were resting and refitting in the Arnhem area when the British 1st Airborne landed during Operation "Market Garden" in September 1944. They fought later in the Ardennes and Hungary, surrendering to U.S. troops in Austria.

10.SS-Panzer-Division "Frundsberg" was raised at the same time as "Hohenstaufen", also from young conscripts. They fought in Russia in early 1944 and France during the summer ending up in Holland during Operation "Market Garden" as well. Sent back to the Eastern Front, they surrendered to the Soviets at Schonau in 1945.

11.SS-Freiwilligen-Panzer-Grenadier-Division "Nordland" was formed in the summer of 1943 from several existing volunteer units. The main one was "Nordland" Regiment from 5.SS-Panzer-Division "Wiking" with SS-Grenadier-Regiment 1 "Danmark" and 3 battalions of SS-Grenadier-Regiment 2 "Norge". In the fall of 1943, it was employed in anti-partisan duty in Croatia and was transferred to the Baltic states, ending up in Berlin in 1945.

A cadre from LAH provided the basis of 12.SS-Panzer-Division "Hitlerjugend" made up primarily of 17 year old members of the Hitler Youth. They developed a ferocious reputation during the battles in Normandy. After fighting their way out of the Falaise Pocket, they were refitted and took part in the Ardennes Offensive. Involved in heavy fighting around Budapest, they marched west to surrender to U.S. forces near Enns, Austria, in 1945.

Throughout 1943, several new Waffen-SS divisions appeared made up of foreign volunteers from conquered lands. In the spring of 1943, 13.Waffen-Gebirgs-Division der SS "Handschar" was raised around a cadre from "Prinz Eugen" recruited mainly from Bosnian Moslems and used in anti-partisan operations in the Balkans. The 14.Waffen-Grenadier-Division der SS (ukrainische Nr.1) was made up of Ukrainians eager to throw off the yoke of Communism. More than 30,000 men volunteered for this unit. The first of two Latvian volunteer units, the 15.Waffen-Grenadier-Division der SS (lettische Nr.1) was originally formed from several internal security units – "Schuma-Bataillone" – in early 1943. It fought in the Baltic states, Poland and Northern Germany.

Himmler's escort battalions was expanded to Sturmbrigade "Reichsführer-SS" in early 1943 and to 16.SS-Panzer-Grenadier-Division "Reichsführer-SS" in October that year. It took part in the occupation of Hungary in March 1944 and in the defensive battles in Italy.

17.SS-Panzer-Grenadier-Division "Götz von Berlichingen" was formed in France in late 1943 with men from training and replacement units, the "Frundsberg" division and "Reichsführer-SS" Assault Brigade plus some Balkan Volksdeutsche. It took part in the defensive battles in Normandy and later in the Alsace region during Operation "Nordwind" in December 1944.

18.SS-Freiwilligen-Panzer-Grenadier-Division "Horst Wessel" was created mainly with Hungarian Volksdeutsche in the spring of 1944. Named after an early "martyr" of the Nazi party, it fought in the Eastern European countries.

There were several other units formed with divisional status although most were not more than battle groups or brigades, while others were divisions on paper only, with a staff and a few units in training. Over a dozen of them were foreign volunteer units organized with Croatian, Estonian, Latvian, Albanian, Hungarian, Dutch, French, Italian and Russian volunteers. Most were commanded by German officers and many were unsuitable for frontline service due to lack of training and equipment.

When WWII ended in Europe, there were almost 100 units organized in the Waffen-SS, large and small. Most were low quality formations and few could be called first class. There were, in fact, very few first rate divisions in the short history of the Waffen-SS, but it was these few that created the elite image of the Waffen-SS that is known to us today.

A two man patrol of SS-Heimwehr Danzig watching the Polish part of the beach in Zoppot (Sopot) between Danzig (Gdansk) and Gdynia during the first few days of the war in September 1939. At this point the border was constructed of barb wire spread over wooden posts in the sand which was intended to make any attack from the direction of Gdynia more difficult for the Poles. Neither soldier has the sleeve eagle common to other SS units and they also have standard Wehrmacht collar patches. This is because SS-Heimwehr Danzig was only partly an SS formation, the largest part of which was created from police units, which since 1938 were under SS control. The soldier nearest to the camera has an Austrian Army entrenching tool on his belt. Note the emblems on the helmets - they are the City of Danzig emblem painted in yellow over a red background.

Three mounted troops from SS-Heimwehr Danzig, including a bugler, crossing the German-Danzig border on September 1, 1939. These soldiers are all from police units involved in the fighting in the Danzig-Gdynia area under SS-Heimwehr Danzig. Many SS and Waffen-SS officers and NCO's served in different levels of SS-Heimwehr Danzig, which was formed from SS-Totenkopf-Sturmbann "Götze" that had been sent to Danzig as a police unit before the war.

SA, SS and Police members crossing the fence around the Polish post office in Danzig during the first day of combat. The SS man seen on the right was a member of the Danziger Allgemeine-SS organized into SS-Abschnitt XXVI and, like most of the organized Nazi units in Danzig (SA men, SS men and even NSDAP members in party uniforms with arm bands), supported SS-Heimwehr Danzig in the fighting in that city.

Two soldiers of SS-Heimwehr Danzig cautiously approach the post office building where the Poles had organized a defense. The building was very strong and the defenders had been armed by the Polish Army and were commanded by ex-Polish Army officers. Almost all of them were civilians, wore no uniforms and fought in a city that did not belong to Poland and so most were executed by the Germans as partisans after their surrender. Three defenders later died as a result of severe wounds.

A 10.5cm leFH18, the standard light howitzer of the German Army, with the barrel in full recoil as it fires a round into the post office building. Note the white letter D painted on the back side of the gun shield, which indicates the fourth gun in the battery. The white spots on the helmets are the Totenkopf emblems.

Men from SS-Heimwehr Danzig approach the post office supported by an ADGZ heavy armored car employed by an Ordnungspolizei armored car platoon. One of fourteen of these Austrian-built armored cars used in Danzig, it carries the police emblem on the turret and SS-runes and the Totenkopf emblem on the hull in addition to the name "Ostmark" painted on the hull sides. Note that the leading SS trooper is wearing only a brown shirt with black trousers and cap. The other men are equipped with the prewar M1916 helmet and tall leather gaiters with short lace up boots.

The final moments of the post office defense. In the foreground is an ADGZ armored car displaying its SS emblems painted on the front and back, while the post office building blazes in the background after a few hours of fighting. The Germans storming the post office had one platoon of 4 ADGZ armored cars at their disposal, however, only one or two were used in this action, the rest being sent to Gdynia.

The battle is over. Police and SS officers view the post office building which has been severely damaged by 10.5cm artillery fire. The SS officer in the middle may be the commander of the SS-Totenkopf-Sturmbann which bore his name.

These SS-Heimwehr Danzig troops dug in at the main square in Gdynia are ready to fight. After the capture of the Polish post office in Danzig, they were sent to fight against Polish forces in Westerplatte and Gdynia where they were also employed in the mass arrests of Polish civilians suspected of anti-German activity. They are heavily equipped but none of them have any Y-straps. Note the emblems painted on the helmets - they are the white deaths head emblem.

Another view of SS-Heimwehr Danzig dug in at Gdynia where they could provide cover fire along the main street through the city. They were armed with a variety of weapons including obsolete WWI vintage machine guns and ineffective 3.7cm PaK 37 anti-tank guns. Note the man posted on the roof of the building in the center of the photo.

Another shot of the same defensive position which covered Swietojanska Street, the main street in the city. The big building seen to the right is the city administration office. Here we see another Maxim MG08, a WWI vintage heavy machine gun.

Soldiers of SS-Heimwehr Danzig remove the emblem of the forest administration and national Piast eagle from a Polish government building in Gdynia as two men from a Police unit look on. They were armed and equipped the same way as most other Wehrmacht and SS units in this period. Such equipment was quite expensive - for example a gas mask cost 22.80 RM, the M1935 helmet 10.80 RM, cartridges for the Mauser rifle 5.60 RM each, bread bag 2.80 RM, water bottle with cup 5.00 RM and mess tin with strap 3.50 RM. Note the numeral "1" on the shoulder straps of the SS-Heimwehr Danzig troops. The rifle carried by the man in the darker uniform is a Mauser 98a and the man just beyond him is equipped with a gas cape contained in the flat bag just above his gas mask case.

A Wehrmacht patrol traveling down the central square in Posen (Poznan) during the first few days of the war in a Strassenpanzerwagen, a commercial vehicle armored for use by the SS police and armed with a Maxim MG08. It carries a two color camouflage scheme with a full set of markings typical for these type of vehicles - a white national cross, the license plate SS 532, an improvised Totenkopf emblem and a white number "1", the exact meaning of which is unknown. There is a small Nazi flag attached to the side and visible to the left of the officer standing in front. It is unknown if this vehicle actually took part in combat and the damage to the front end was likely caused by an accident.

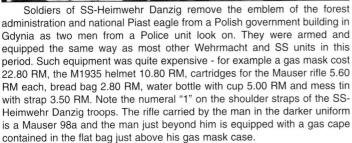

Hitler among the soldiers of a second line unit behind the front during the first days of September 1939. His back is protected by an SS guard, selected from the best members of the LAH Regiment, who traveled together with him across the Polish battlefields during that time, when he was constantly on the move by car and train. Note the two SS bodyguards do not have the standard SS-runes on their collar patches. There are many instances when SS soldiers wore non-standard or no patches against authorized orders or regulations.

A heavily retouched photo of men of 1.SS-Kavallerie-Brigade traveling down a village road in Poland during the autumn of 1939. This unit took part in second line duties against Polish partisans and the expulsion of the non-German population from the new territories incorporated into the Third Reich.

A group of soldiers from LAH dig in not far from Warsaw, sometime in mid-September 1939. Note the unusual style of camouflage straps seen on the helmet of the man standing and the light colored cuffbands on both the men to the right.

Another retouched photo of police troops during a meal break in October/November 1939, while taking part in action against one of the many Polish villages pacified by the Germans. The heaviest actions had been launched throughout the first month of the war when resistance had been the strongest and Poland was still under military rule. The main forces employed in these actions were police battalions and regiments supported by about a dozen Totenkopf regiments. Note the soldier on the extreme right - he is one of the NSKK volunteers from Berlin who joined the police troops as a motorcyclist in the almost completely non-motorized police units.

A mounted patrol, commanded by an SS-Unterscharführer, composed of young candidates for the SS, members of the quasi-military youth organization, Hitlerjugend. They are wearing military uniforms typical for the NSKK with a sleeve eagle but without collar patches. The armbands on their left arms indicate they belong to the HJ organization.

An SS police troop during anti-partisan training along the edge of a pine forest. The soldier closest to the camera is armed with the rare MP28 usually issued to second line or police troops. The officer is wearing a black leather overcoat which was to become a trademark symbol of the Gestapo.

A close-up photo of two soldiers from SS-Regiment "Westland" during training. The closest man appears to be wearing a checked civilian shirt under his tunic. This regiment was formed on May 25, 1940 from volunteers in occupied Holland and Flanders and together with SS-Regiment "Nordland", was later that year grouped with SS-Regiment "Germania" to form SS-Division "Wiking".

Another photo of this group of soldiers showing an NCO machine gunner watching enemy positions through his field glasses. He is armed with the Czech manufactured ZB-26, designated MG26 (t) by the Germans, which was used by many SS police units. Both these shots were probably taken during anti-partisan training for police employed in occupation duties in Poland.

Men of SS-Standarte "Germania" in Holland or France in May 1940. Though widely used by SS troops in this campaign, only one man appears to have a camouflage smock and it is tucked under his belt. The SS-Unterscharführer on the right has applied mud to his helmet as camouflage. The man on the left is carrying a tripod which is used to set up their MG34 for use in the anti-aircraft role. In December that year, this unit was transferred to the newly formed SS-Division "Germania" which was renamed "Wiking" a few weeks later.

SS-Verfügungsdivision (later SS-Division "Das Reich") commander, SS-Gruppenführer Paul Hausser discusses the battle situation with one of his officers in France, May 1940. Affectionately called "Papa" by his men, Hausser was the first commander of this division after its creation in 1939. In August 1941, he was awarded the Knights Cross for his successful leadership during the early phase of the war in Russia. In July 1943 he received the Oakleaves and in August 1944 the Swords, as commander of 7.Armee.

Men of SS-Verfügungsdivision in a victory parade across a bridge at Hendaye on the French-Spanish border, July 9, 1940. Leading the parade are three SS-Untersturmführer including a standard bearer wearing large white gloves and a gorget around his neck. The other two men have both been awarded the Iron Cross First Class.

Adolf Hitler inspecting a French Char B1 bis heavy tank knocked out by the Germans somewhere in France, 1940. Behind, to his right, is Reichsführer-SS Heinrich Himmler along with Himmler's adjutant, SS-Gruppenführer Karl Wolff over his left shoulder. Hitler's SS adjutant, SS-Untersturmführer Hansgeorg Schultze is the young officer to Himmler's right.

Another trip by Hitler to the French battlefield, this time to one of the fortifications on the Maginot Line accompanied by a large group of officers from the SS, Wehrmacht, Luftwaffe and Polizei. In the center of the photograph, Colonel-General Wilhelm Keitel is speaking to Luftwaffe Hauptmann Nicolaus von Below, Hitler's Luftwaffe adjutant, while his SS adjutant, SS-Untersturmführer Hansgeorg Schultze is visible over Keitel's right shoulder. Heinrich Himmler's profile can be seen just over Hitler's right shoulder while Martin Bormann is on the extreme left.

SS-Obergruppenführer "Sepp" Dietrich during an inspection of LAH by General Johannes Blaskowitz, February 1941. LSSAH was considered to be an elite unit and Himmler did much to promote this ideal throughout the SS units. He claimed the Waffen-SS to be the elite of the Nazi movement and of the military forces of the Third Reich. LAH was originally formed in 1933 as Hitler's personal bodyguard. The tank visible to the right is a Pz.Kpfw.I Ausf.B.

Dietrich leaving the HQ of his LAH at the Hotel Acropole in Athens, Greece, April 1941. The soldier guarding the entrance is wearing the field gray version of the black panzer uniform issued to LAH assault gun crews for the Balkans campaign. He is also wearing ankle boots and canvas gaiters which were very rare for this period. Several divisional command pennants are visible, one in the doorway, two mounted on the vehicle and one painted on the mudguard which consist of a black over white over red stripe. The one painted on the mudguard also indicates the staff of a motorized division. LAH was not elevated to the status of a panzer division until October 22, 1943.

SS-Hauptsturmführer Fritz Klingenberg, one of the best known heroes of the Waffen-SS during the Balkan campaign, speaking on a radio broadcast about his capture of the city of Belgrade. All three of the soldiers are wearing the Feldmutze cap with slightly different details. Klingenberg's cap is the standard army pattern with the Nazi eagle on the front, silver braid around the top and front of the turn-up, inverted "V" waffenfarbe (soutache) but with a silver Totenkopf pin instead of the sewn on embroidered Totenkopf. The SS-Scharführer on the right has the SS pattern cap with an embroidered SS eagle on a black triangular patch on the side of the turn-up and an embossed Totenkopf on a matt gray button on the front under the soutache. The officer holding the microphone also has the army pattern cap but without the soutache. His early "Palm" pattern camouflage smock is fitted with a zipper and also has two white stripes on each sleeve, an early form of identification. NCOs had one stripe, officers had two and field grade officers had three. Note also the absence of collar patches on Klingenberg's uniform and the Wehrmacht style eagle insignia on his left sleeve.

The military action over, the job of cleaning up and maintaining Nazi policies in the conquered lands fell to the Ordnungspolizei, here photographed in the company of SS-Gruppenführer Kurt Daluege on the right. Daluege, nicknamed "Dummi-Dummi" because of his limited intelligence, was an early member of the Nazi party and was appointed Chief of Security Police in 1936. This photo was taken in Slovenia in early May 1941 during a visit to the police units involved in the Balkans. The Ordnungspolizei were created in the early 1920s as a way of increasing the strength of the military beyond the limits imposed by the allies after WWI and was later on taken over by the SS when Himmler was given command of all German police units in 1934. Their uniforms were similar to those of the SS and Wehrmacht and differed only in minor details such as the cuffs and insignia.

A group of LAH soldiers in camouflage smocks photographed during an excursion somewhere among the ruins of Olympia after the Greek surrender in May 1941.

SS soldiers inspecting a bunker abandoned by Soviet troops during the first days of Barbarossa in June 1941, which involved all of the units of the SS, over 200,000 men in all.

An SS-NCO, perhaps a war artist, sketches on a drawing board while seated in the remains of a damaged Soviet Polikarpov I-16 fighter plane in June 1941. His collar has the white NCO braid around it but the SS runes on his collar patches appear to be a dark gray color.

A traditionally valuable war prize, an enemy flag - here the banner of a Soviet military formation with the slogan "To fight for Lenin's - Stalin's cause be ready!" - was captured by these men of SS-Division "Reich" in July 1941. The civilian at left is providing a translation of the meaning to them. Members of a reconnaissance unit, these men all wear camouflage smocks and helmet covers with a summer "Plane Tree" pattern with light green, dark green and light brown colors.

A combat council attended by Wehrmacht, Luftwaffe and SS officers. The SS-Obersturmführer, an experienced officer decorated with the black Wound Badge for 1-2 wounds and silver General Assault Badge, is wearing the M37 officer's tunic with the SS pattern Feldmütze complete with all the standard SS insignia.

15

Soldiers of SS-Division "Nord" (later 6.SS-Gebirgs-Division "Nord") in the Northern Soviet Union in 1941. They are wearing early pattern camouflage smocks and helmet covers in a "Plane Tree" pattern with field gray trousers tucked into puttees over lace up ankle boots which is typical for this unit at this time. Four of the men are equipped with mosquito nets pushed back up over their helmets. In the foreground is an MG26(t) and the soldiers are posed around a 3.7cm PaK 36 anti-tank gun with a white number "7" painted on the rear side of the gun shield. The man standing in the rear is also wearing a wide leather bandolier used by artillery crews to move their gun.

SS men from the same unit marching down a road through a field in the Soviet Union. The two-man machine gun team is carrying another Czech produced weapon, the MG37(t) (ZB37). The overall weight of this weapon was 19kg so it was not easy to carry. The camouflage smock worn by the soldier carrying the machine gun is an early "Palm" pattern which had been widely distributed by the time of the invasion of Russia. Another MG26(t) for anti-aircraft defense is mounted on the cross country car used by the troop commander.

Soldiers from SS-Division "Totenkopf" struggle to move a BMW R12 motorcycle combination bogged down in a soft, sandy road somewhere in the Soviet Union in the early autumn of 1941. The motorcycle, driven by an SS-Rottenführer who is wearing the Iron Cross Second Class ribbon, is marked with a tactical sign of the 13th company of a motorized infantry division and carries the white Totenkopf emblem painted on the side of the front mudguard along with a white number "23" or "25" on the side of the gas tank.

A similar situation, but this time the SS crew of this BMW R61 or R66 motorcycle combination has run into problems with mud. As can be seen by the collar patches, this SS-Sturmann is also from SS-Division "Totenkopf". Note the unusual tactical markings painted on the front of the sidecar. There is an "s" painted above the symbol for the second company of divisional services.

Members of various arms of service having a conversation somewhere in the Soviet Union in 1941. The four soldiers on the left are from the Wehrmacht "French Volunteer Legion" which passed to Waffen-SS command in August 1943. The national shield emblem was then moved over to the left sleeve keeping with the practice of the SS to display their insignia opposite to the Wehrmacht. Also visible in this photo is an SS-Sturmann and a Luftwaffe Feldwebel on the extreme right.

An SS soldier examines a captured Soviet mine in September 1941. His uniform is a little irregular in that he is wearing a heavy wool sweater instead of his field uniform tunic under his early "Plane Tree" pattern camouflage smock. His helmet has been painted with a light coat of camouflage paint that is beginning to show signs of wear.

A group of SS pass through a burning Russian village with their two 7.5cm leFH 18 light howitzers being towed by horses in a quite unusual manner. Ropes have been attached to the axles of the gun's wheels and are being towed facing forward. The gun trails are being supported off the ground by two men aided by another man and some boxes of ammunition as a counterweight on the front. Note the number of stick hand grenades carried by these men.

The same group of soldiers photographed marching through the village led by an SS-Untersturmführer. Many of the men in these two photographs are wearing spurs which indicates they are from the SS-Kavallerie-Brigade. Initially, this unit was used behind the front lines to mop up pockets of Russian resistance bypassed by the rapid advances of the German Army.

These men looking over the city of Odessa just after its capture in October 1941, are likely members of Einsatzgruppe D. This city of half a million people had a large population of Jews and so the soldiers of these units had much to do. The Einsatzgruppe members came mostly from the different police units - the Gestapo and SD who were employed in rounding up the victims - and the Ordnungspolizei who manned the firing squads. Note the details of the MP28 being carried by the man on the left and the motorcycle coat worn by the man on the right.

On leaving the village, the SS troops were fired on forcing the men to seek cover in a ditch near the road. These photos were taken in August 1941.

A 7.5cm leIG 18 in action against Soviet defense positions in a village set ablaze by artillery fire in October 1941. SS-Division "Reich" led the attack toward Moscow in November 1941 coming within a few miles of the city. The Russian winter counteroffensive employing the Siberian divisions inflicted severe casualties on "Reich" - almost 11,000 men by the middle of February 1942. In May 1942, it was renamed SS-Division "Das Reich".

A group of SS soldiers travel across the Russian landscape in their Horch Kfz.15 personnel car in late October 1941. The vehicle is an overall gray color that has been covered in dust and mud. The man closest to the camera is wearing the wide leather artillery bandolier as well.

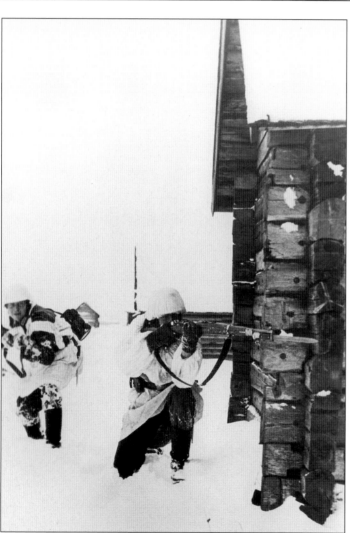

A couple of soldiers from the Polizei-Division, note the army style collar patches and SS sleeve eagle on the man on the left, take up a position behind a farmhouse in the Leningrad area in January 1942. The winter camouflage smocks were specially made for the SS whereas the Wehrmacht had none and their men commonly used bed sheets as a temporary expedient. Both of these men are wearing them over their uniforms without the greatcoat underneath.

SS-Oberführer Max Simon, wearing the rubberized motorcycle coat, presents the Iron Cross Second Class to the brave soldiers of SS-Division "Totenkopf" which had been encircled for several months in the "Demyansk Pocket" in the winter of 1941-42. Note the officer standing behind is wearing a variation of the uniform sometimes seen in this division - Totenkopf emblems on both collar patches. Simon later commanded 16.SS-Panzer-Grenadier-Division "Reichsführer-SS"

20

Soldiers of SS-Division "Wiking" marching across the oilfields near Taganrog in 1942 during "Fall Blau", the German summer offensive into the Caucasus. During their retreat, the Soviets set fire to the wells and storage tanks to deny them to the Germans. Although motorized, "Wiking" was poorly equipped for this operation. SS-Division "Leibstandarte Adolf Hitler" and "Reich" were pulled from the front for refitting and did not participate.

After the German-Finnish agreement of June 1941, the Finnisches-Freiwilligen-Bataillon der Waffen-SS was raised with about 421 men. The size of the battalion grew to over 1000 men and, in 1942, was absorbed into SS-Division "Wiking", and fought on the Eastern Front for the duration of the war. Here we see troops from this unit picking up their personal equipment from a transport truck.

SS soldiers marching through a village in the central Soviet Union during anti-partisan action in late fall of 1942. These men are also lacking full equipment such as "Y" straps, mess tins, Zeltbahns and even water bottles. The two soldiers closest to the camera do not have gas masks either but are equipped with the M1939 pack frame for carrying heavier pieces of equipment on their backs such as the 5cm mortar ammunition boxes seen here.

An MG34 machine gun team under light artillery fire from partisans in the spring or summer of 1943. It is worth noting that neither man is fully equipped except for entrenching tools, gas masks and the spare machine gun barrel case carried by the man closest to the camera. During the first 1 1/2 years of the war in Russia, the first SS divisions had become better equipped and armed than most Wehrmacht divisions while the newer ones were often more poorly equipped.

This photo shows SS-Sturmbannführer Jorgen Bakke, commander of Freiwilligen Legion Niederland walking through a trench somewhere on the Eastern Front where it fought throughout 1942. In July 1943, it was expanded into 4.SS-Freiwilligen-Panzer-Grenadier-Brigade "Nederland". Though not completely visible, the inscription on his cuffband reads "Frw. Legion Niederland".

A soldier from an unknown SS unit viewing the battlefield through a scissors periscope during the winter of 1942-43. He is wearing an army pattern winter snow suit, field gray on one side and white on the other. Note the unusual variation of the Totenkopf emblem on the front of his field cap - it is missing the crossed bones.

An SS-Unterscharführer leading a column of SS soldiers from an unknown SS-Gebirgs-Division on a training exercise during the winter of 1942-43. The mountain divisions were employed mainly in anti-partisan duties where their mountain climbing and skiing skills were never utilized to their full potential. Note the skis and poles are painted white which helped camouflage the soldiers when properly uniformed and equipped.

Heavily loaded with winter equipment, SS troops march across an open field in the Soviet Union in January 1943. They are wearing one piece snow overalls that were normally issued to Wehrmacht troops and the felt and leather winter boots. They are also wearing fur lined caps without any insignia that were similar to Soviet ones. It is worth noting that they are all carrying packs containing their personal belongings that were normally transported by supply vehicles.

Staff officers of SS-Kavallerie-Division review their situation on a map board during anti-partisan action in February 1943. The officer is wearing the fur lined anorak that had just been introduced along with a colorful pair of civilian mitts. On August 2, 1941, SS-Kavallerie-Regiment 1 and 2 combined to form SS-Kavallerie-Brigade with SS-Standartenführer Hermann Fegelein as commander. The Brigade began mopping up operations in the rear of the central sector of the Eastern Front and continued with this duty until late 1942. On October 22, 1943, it was reformed as 8.SS-Kavallerie-Division.

An SS machine gun troop heavily loaded with boxes of ammunition, combat equipment and blankets photographed during a march break near the front lines in early 1943. The vast expanses of the Russian landscape made supply to the troops difficult which resulted in the men having to carry most of what they needed with them wherever they went.

Men of SS-Panzer-Grenadier-Division "Das Reich" entering Kharkov in March 1943. These young SS men are riding on a Pz.Kpfw.III Ausf.M and are wearing the fur lined anorak. At this time the ranks of the SS were being filled out with 17-18 year old boys who were put into front line service with only 6-12 months training. Their lack of experience sometimes resulted in unnecessary casualties during combat, especially in the autumn of 1943, when the SS were used as fire brigades throughout the front. The tank turret visible in the foreground is from a Pz.Kpfw.IV.

A Kfz.15 heavy cross country car with the tactical sign of SS-Panzer-Grenadier-Division "Das Reich" on its left mudguard in the Kharkov area, where the SS fought one of its finest battles, in March 1943. The vehicle with license plate SS-500594 has a Nazi flag draped across the engine compartment for air identification, a common practice during offensive operations. The Wehrmacht soldier on the left is wearing a white winter hood while the two SS soldiers on the right are wearing white winter two piece camouflage suits over their fur lined anoraks along with a colored arm band on the left sleeve. In warmer spring weather, these suits became very dirty which reduced their effectiveness. Standing orders dictated they be used only when weather conditions were suitable, but it was often not practical to follow at all times.

Two officers and men of SS-Panzer-Grenadier-Division "Totenkopf" photographed on a Pz.Kpfw.IV in the center of Kharkov in March 1943, just after the recapture of the city. The SS-Untersturmführer tank commander is wearing a sleeveless sheepskin jacket over his black panzer uniform. The other men wear the fur-lined anorak.

One of the many T-26 tanks captured during the first year of the war against the Soviets. These tanks were put into service in second line units such as the Ordnungspolizei or other SS police formations, to fight against partisan movements through occupied Eastern Europe. This T-26 was employed against Polish underground forces in the early spring of 1943 in the Zamojszczyzna area. It has been repainted in dark gray and carries national crosses and the tactical sign for an armored formation.

SS-Unterscharführer, Eastern Front 1942

Only the camouflage helmet cover and belt buckle identify this motorcyclist as a member of the Waffen-SS. The golden yellow piping on his shoulder board further identifies him as belonging to a motorized reconnaissance unit. Until June 1942 the piping would have been copper brown.

The waterproof motorcycle coat was a popular and practical item. Originally introduced for army motorcyclist, the 'Kradschutzmantel' was soon adopted by the SS. Despite regulations restricting its use to authorized personnel, it was a much prized acquisition for general wear particularly by officers.

It was made of field grey rubberized cotton twill with all seams waterproofed. The collar was faced with field grey wool although early examples were dark blue/green. The double-breasted design was generously cut and was intended to be worn over equipment (contemporary photos tend to show otherwise). An overlapping pleated panel in back allowed some ventilation. The half belt in back could allow some adjustment of the waist. With the back vent reaching almost to the waist, the lower panels could be wrapped around the legs and buttoned in place providing superior weather protection. A pair of large pockets with buttoned flaps were located in front. It should be noted that not all coats had provision for attaching shoulder straps.

Motorcyclists were issued various types of goggles - presumably whatever was available. In this case, aviators' type is worn. The gauntlets are the standard pattern made from heavy field grey cotton duck. Grey leather is used for the palm, thumb and separate fingers as well for the adjustment straps on the back.

Only the magazine pouches for his slung MP40 and a M1935 dispatch case are worn on the belt. Leather marching boots are visible beneath the long coat.

VOLSTAD 99

SS-Reiter, SS Cavalry Division, Eastern Front 1942

This is the typical image of Waffen-SS mounted personnel from 1942 to 1945. The uniform is the same as that worn by dismounted troops with the exception of riding breeches and high leather riding boots with spurs. The field grey breeches have a leather seat reinforcement in shades of grey or brown. Late production examples had this reinforcement made from field grey cloth.

Over the M-1940 field blouse is worn a camouflage smock M-1940 in 'Palm Tree' pattern. It was very much the fashion to wear the early style smock with both cuffs and skirt tucked back under the elastic.

Issue of the camouflage cap officially began in the summer of 1942 and it quickly became a popular and functional item. Typically there were variations with most having a central seam along the top panel and ventilation holes were not always present. While fully reversible, the 'autumn' side had all the exposed seams; most notably around the lower edge.

Subdued insignia were authorized for a brief period in late 1942 but this was quickly rescinded.

Standard equipment for a rifleman was provided with the usual belt and cartridge pouches. The bread bag and field flask were worn in the normal position, however, the bayonet and shovel (if worn - it was sometimes fastened to the saddle) were carried on the right rather than the usual left side. The purpose was to prevent the Kar 98k - slung over the right shoulder - from striking these items. Accordingly, the gas mask canister was slung over the left shoulder and positioned rather high on the right side. Cavalry pattern belt support straps were used since mounted personnel did not require the 'D' rings and pack straps needed by dismounted troops. In fact, the right saddlebag M-1934 had integral carrying straps and could be used as a pack when necessary.

The saddle is the Army Model 1925 (Armeesattel 25). The saddlebags M-1934 (Packtasche 34) are attached to a coupling device which is then fastened to the saddle. Suspended from the left rear of the saddle is a carbine carrying device (a similar scabbard was provided for the MG34). However, the carbine 'bucket' saw limited use since the rifle could be just as easily slung across the back. On the rear of the saddle, the zeltbahn, overcoat and a blanket might be strapped. The mess tin was commonly strapped to the right saddlebag. His helmet was frequently strapped to the ring behind the right skirt leather. The left saddlebag was for care of the horse while the right side was for the cavalryman.

VOLSTAD99

SS-Sturmann, 7.Freiwilligen-Gebirgs-Division 'Prinz Eugen', Yugoslavia 1944 (7th Volunteer Mountain Division 'Prinz Eugen')

This 'Volunteer' wears the standard Waffen-SS field grey uniform of the period. The standard M-43 field cap had by now replaced the mountain cap and from October 1943, the 'Edelweiss' flower could be applied to the left side.

The SS did wear army issue uniforms and uniforms produced specifically for the Waffen-SS followed the design changes of the army version. However, the M-43 field blouse of the SS had a front closure with five buttons - the army tunic had six buttons. As the Waffen-SS was not recognized as part of the official German armed forces, they were not entitled to wear the national emblem on the right chest - instead it was displayed on the left sleeve. Out of view on his upper right arm was another 'Edelweiss' embroidered on an oval patch. The right collar patch bears the 'Odal' rune unique to 'Prinz Eugen' division. The cuff title as well is worn on the left sleeve. The left collar patch along with the chevron indicates his rank. In his second buttonhole is the ribbon of the Iron Cross 2nd Class. The Infantry Assault Badge is pinned to his left pocket. The black shoulder straps bear only the light green piping of mountain troops.

By 1944, the 'Keilhose' trousers had largely replaced the mountain trousers. Rugged lace-up mountain boots remained standard though. The heavy, studded construction provided support and protection in difficult terrain and the boots were much favored by other than mountain troops. The original elasticated puttees were now commonly replaced by issue canvas gaiters.

The usual rifleman's belt and Kar 98k pouches are worn with the bread bag and bayonet in normal positions. The integral hooks of the field blouse provided support assisted by internal cloth straps that helped to distribute the weight. The shoulder straps of the M-1931 rucksack had adjustable hooks that could be hooked into the `D' rings of the pouches. The rucksack carried the soldier's requirements on longer patrols. Underneath the flap of the pack is his 'blurred edge' smock with his helmet strapped to the outside. The water bottle would normally be the larger 1 liter type rather than the standard .8 liter version.

VOLSTAD99

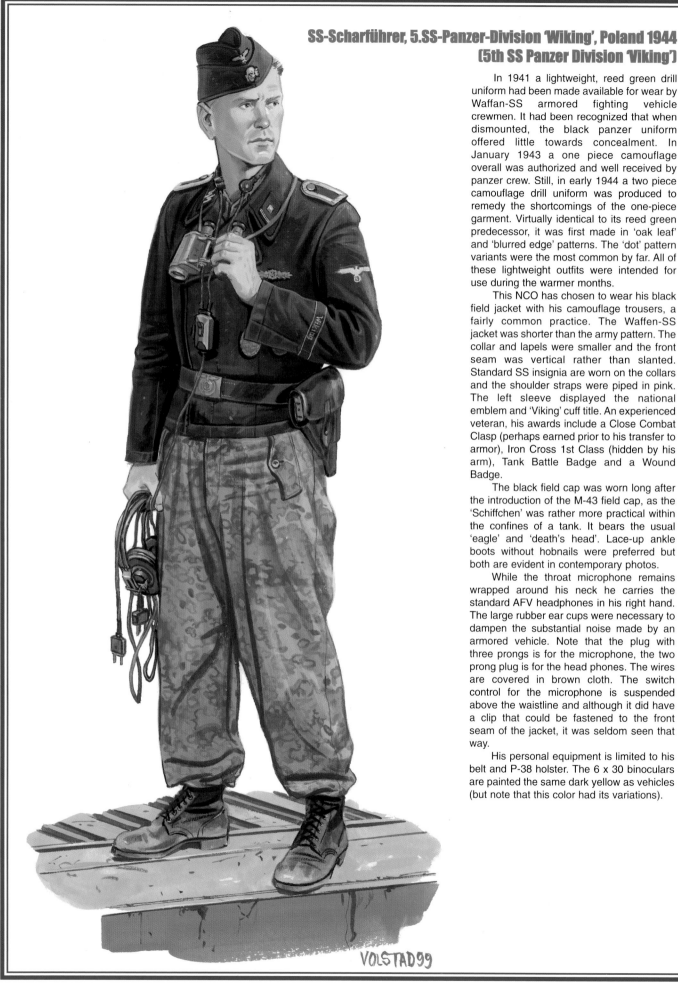

SS-Scharführer, 5.SS-Panzer-Division 'Wiking', Poland 1944 (5th SS Panzer Division 'Viking')

In 1941 a lightweight, reed green drill uniform had been made available for wear by Waffan-SS armored fighting vehicle crewmen. It had been recognized that when dismounted, the black panzer uniform offered little towards concealment. In January 1943 a one piece camouflage overall was authorized and well received by panzer crew. Still, in early 1944 a two piece camouflage drill uniform was produced to remedy the shortcomings of the one-piece garment. Virtually identical to its reed green predecessor, it was first made in 'oak leaf' and 'blurred edge' patterns. The 'dot' pattern variants were the most common by far. All of these lightweight outfits were intended for use during the warmer months.

This NCO has chosen to wear his black field jacket with his camouflage trousers, a fairly common practice. The Waffen-SS jacket was shorter than the army pattern. The collar and lapels were smaller and the front seam was vertical rather than slanted. Standard SS insignia are worn on the collars and the shoulder straps were piped in pink. The left sleeve displayed the national emblem and 'Viking' cuff title. An experienced veteran, his awards include a Close Combat Clasp (perhaps earned prior to his transfer to armor), Iron Cross 1st Class (hidden by his arm), Tank Battle Badge and a Wound Badge.

The black field cap was worn long after the introduction of the M-43 field cap, as the 'Schiffchen' was rather more practical within the confines of a tank. It bears the usual 'eagle' and 'death's head'. Lace-up ankle boots without hobnails were preferred but both are evident in contemporary photos.

While the throat microphone remains wrapped around his neck he carries the standard AFV headphones in his right hand. The large rubber ear cups were necessary to dampen the substantial noise made by an armored vehicle. Note that the plug with three prongs is for the microphone, the two prong plug is for the head phones. The wires are covered in brown cloth. The switch control for the microphone is suspended above the waistline and although it did have a clip that could be fastened to the front seam of the jacket, it was seldom seen that way.

His personal equipment is limited to his belt and P-38 holster. The 6 x 30 binoculars are painted the same dark yellow as vehicles (but note that this color had its variations).

VOLSTAD 99

A Pz.Kpfw.38 (t) Ausf.G painted in overall sand, in the streets of Warsaw during the Jewish Ghetto uprising in the spring of 1943. The police and SS units storming the Ghetto were supported by obsolete tanks produced by the Czechs, Germans and Italians.

Transport trains of SS-Kavallerie-Division traveling through a Russian village in June 1943. This was the only real cavalry unit in the SS for most of the war. 22.Freiwilligen-Kavallerie-Division der SS and 33.Waffen-Kavallerie-Division der SS were hastily assembled, under-strength units formed late in the war mostly from Hungarian cavalry forces. 37.SS-Freiwilligen-Kavallerie-Division "Lützow" was formed from the remnants of 8. and 22.SS-Kavallerie-Divisions in February-March 1945. Cavalry unit were generally not suitable for fighting in urban areas and were used mostly behind the front engaged in anti-partisan duties in open rural areas.

SS soldiers give aid to an injured Soviet pilot after his obsolete Polikarpov U-2 plane used for daytime reconnaissance and night bombing missions was shot down. The manner in which the soldier stepping over the pilot is wearing his gas mask suggests these men are from a motorcycle reconnaissance unit. They are all wearing the early style "Palm" pattern camouflage smock. The soldier kneeling on the right is wearing a camouflage field cap introduced in June 1942.

NSKK soldiers supported by a captured BA10 Model 1937 heavy armored car during anti-partisan actions in a forest in the central Soviet Union in June 1943. The vehicle, which originally belonged to an SS police unit, is painted with a green camouflage pattern over the sand background and has national crosses painted on the sides and on top of the engine compartment. A vehicle name has been painted on the side under the open visor and the unit emblem, a winged sword, painted on the front.

Another Soviet victim falls from the sky onto the flat Russian steppe as a group of soldiers rush to capture him. The flak units of the Waffen-SS divisions did not have much work to do up until mid-1943 because the Luftwaffe controlled the skies over the Soviet Union without much trouble. For example, during "Operation Zitadelle", when this photo was taken, through the first week of the battle only a handful of Soviet planes were brought down over German territory, however, dozens were intercepted and shot down by German fighters over Soviet controlled territory. The strength of SS anti-aircraft units grew rapidly after June 1941. There were only 79 guns and 2,000 men at the end of 1941 but by the end of 1943, this had grown to 1,118 guns and over 21,000 men.

Another two Soviet airmen taken into captivity by SS troops, probably during "Operation Zitadelle" in July 1943. The panzer crewman standing on the left is wearing the new camouflage summer coverall in the "Plane Tree" pattern which was issued to tank and armored car crews to replace the black panzer uniform in the spring. Note there are two buttons on the pocket flap which normally only had one.

Soldiers from the same unit advancing through the field of sunflowers in pursuit of the enemy forces. The man nearest the camera is wearing an early style "Plane Tree" pattern camouflage smock.

This photograph illustrates how effective the SS camouflage smocks and helmet covers were. Since 1941, uniform insignia was produced in a dull gray color so as not to compromise the camouflage, as can be seen by the SS runes on the collar of the man on the right. In this photo, showing anti-partisan action prior to "Operation Zitadelle" at the end of June 1943, we can see SS soldiers approaching an enemy village through a field of sunflowers.

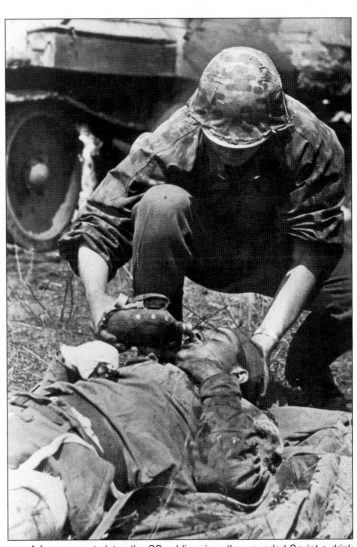

An SS soldier stands by while a Soviet infantryman tends to a wounded comrade in early July 1943, while the remains of a T-34/76 Model 1943 blazes in the background. The SS soldier is lightly equipped - he does not even carry spare ammunition for his MP40.

A few moments later, the SS soldier gives the wounded Soviet a drink of water from his M1931 field flask. He has a well worn "Plane Tree" pattern camouflage helmet cover and an early style "Palm" pattern camouflage smock, originally introduced in 1940.

An interesting photo of three SS officers conferring with HQ on a field telephone. The SS-Hauptsturmführer with the telephone is wearing a non-regulation tunic made from Wehrmacht "Splinter" pattern Zeltbahn material. Just as unusual, the officer on the left is wearing one made from SS "Palm" pattern camouflage material with a "Blurred Edge" pattern helmet cover. Both are wearing them over their standard issue shirts. The officer on the right is wearing an early style "Palm" pattern smock with the two white bars indicating the wearer is an officer.

Soldiers from SS-Kavallerie-Division uncover a cache of weapons and ammunition left behind by the retreating Soviets. These men are all dressed typically for this period with early style "Plane Tree" pattern camouflage smocks over their standard field gray uniform and all but one is wearing the camouflage field cap. Camouflage pattern trousers were not introduced until later with the two piece reversible snow suit, white on one side with a camouflage print on the other.

Waiting for orders. A group of SS soldiers rest in a ditch during the fighting around Belgorod in July 1943. The Torn.Fu.f radio set seen on the left was the standard field radio used by assault troops in place of the field telephone which required the laying of phone lines. Fast and simple battlefield communications were important and was one of the ways that gave the Germans superiority over Soviet troops.

An SS crew replenish their Tiger's ammunition through the loader's hatch in the turret roof. Both men wear the one piece camouflage coveralls with the camouflage field cap. The 8.8cm rounds have colored projectiles for quick identification during battle conditions. The shells with the markings "Pzgr.39" and "FES" are armor piercing and the tip is painted black. The other shells are probably high explosive which were normally carried in equal quantities. The shell casings may also be lacquered steel instead of brass.

The Pz.Kpfw.VI Tiger I Ausf.E, one of the most effective weapons used by the Germans during "Operation Zitadelle", is seen here advancing across a vast grain field in the Belgorod area prior to the battle. All three SS-Panzer-Grenadier-Divisions taking part in this attack were equipped with a company of these heavy tanks, which made them more powerful than most Panzer divisions of the Wehrmacht. Each company was equipped with 13 to 15 tigers. This Tiger is from SS-Panzer-Grenadier-Division "Das Reich".

A Pz.Kpfw.III Ausf.N of SS-Panzer-Grenadier-Division "Totenkopf" struggling through a muddy river crossing north of Belgorod. It is painted in overall sand which has been covered by mud on the lower hull. The divisional emblem, created for "Operation Zitadelle" is painted on the front of the hull beside the driver's visor and consists of three vertical white bars. In the background, another Pz.Kpfw.III can be seen along with an Sd.Kfz.250, three Sd.Kfz.251s, four Opel Maultiers and a Krupp Protz Kfz.81 towing a 2cm FlaK 36 anti-aircraft gun plus a few other miscellaneous vehicles.

The SS units had to fight partisans as well as Soviet front line troops during "Operation Zitadelle" in July 1943. Here we see an SS motorcycle company in action against partisans in a village behind the front. These two Zundapp KS750 motorcycle combinations are heavily stowed with the belongings of the crews rolled up neatly with Zeltbahn shelter quarters.

Yak-1 fighter plane of the Soviet Air Force shot down in the Belgorod area being inspected by SS soldiers looking for souvenirs.

Tanks from an SS division marching in the direction of the front lines. The nearest tank is a Pz.Kpfw.III Ausf.M with a full set of armored side skirts and camouflaged with green spots over the sand background. The tactical number "06" in red with a white outline indicates a staff vehicle. The "0" beside it is white with a thin black outline. In front are the more powerful Pz.Kpfw.IV Ausf.H armed with the 7.5cm L/48 gun.

August 1943 – heavy fighting in the Kursk Bulge destroyed many buildings and brought much captured equipment to the Germans – here a 2 - ton Studebaker truck, built in the U.S. and sent to the Soviet Union under the Lend-Lease Act of 1940. It was an excellent vehicle and was well liked by all who used it including Americans, Poles, Commonwealth forces and the Soviets. The vehicle in the lead is a Mercedes-Benz L1500A personnel carrier.

Various tanks, armored and unarmored half-tracks and personnel carriers are spread out across the Russian steppe to present a smaller target in case of bombing or heavy artillery fire.

SS troops in a Polish village in the summer of 1943. The man standing in the middle is wearing a Model 1942 type 1 camouflage smock in the "Oak Leaf" pattern and the others wear the M44 camouflage drill uniform in the "Dot" and "Oak Leaf" patterns. The man on the right appears to have his NCO shoulder straps on his uniform. In the background, an Sd.Kfz.11 half-track prime mover towing a 7.5cm PaK40 anti-tank gun can be seen.

A Pz.Kpfw.III Ausf.J armed with the 5cm L/42 gun passes by an SS anti-tank position during Soviet offensive operations in the Belgorod area in late August or early September 1943. The heavily camouflaged gun appears to be a 7.5cm PaK 40. The man on the left is wearing an early style "Palm" pattern camouflage smock while the others have "Plane Tree" or "Oak Leaf" patterns - there are very few photographs that show "Palm" pattern helmet covers.

Men of an SS MG42 machine gun team climb aboard a Pz.Kpfw.IV Ausf.G which, judging by the small box with the national cross painted on, belongs to SS-Panzer-Grenadier-Division "Leibstandarte Adolf Hitler". A machine gun crew usually consisted of five men - the squad leader, machine gunner, and ammunition feeder plus two infantrymen to help carry spare ammunition. The man closest to the camera is carrying a spare barrel container on his back.

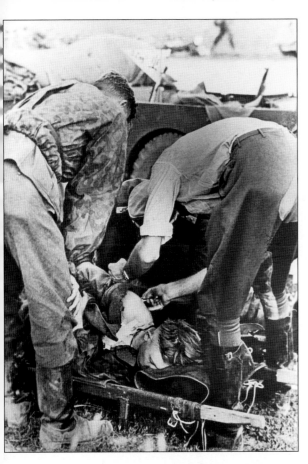

SS soldiers of a motorcycle company watch a landing Feisler Fi 156 "Storch" light plane with the code DM + BK under the wings and fitted with a water tank on the underside of the fuselage. The motorcycles are BMW R75 combinations. These men may be messengers waiting for orders arriving on this plane.

A medical officer attends to a wounded SS soldier who has been shot through the chest. He is wearing privately purchased officer's trousers with leather reinforced legs and officer's riding boots. The SS soldier on the left is wearing an early style "Plane Tree" pattern camouflage smock.

These SS soldiers have dug themselves into the side of an anti-tank ditch to afford better protection from shell splinters. They are all armed with the Mauser 98k rifle and hand grenades. The two MG ammunition boxes are being used to hold additional rounds for their rifles. Very often, this extra ammunition available to the Germans helped turn back Soviet assaults. The Russians were never supplied with enough ammunition and had to choose their targets carefully in order to avoid running out early in the battle.

After the collapse of Mussolini's Fascist Regime in late July 1943, Hitler sent 1.SS-Panzer-Division "Leibstandarte Adolf Hitler" to northern Italy with orders to react swiftly and decisively to any action that would affect the German positions there. Here we see a column of Steyr 1500A heavy personnel cars of LAH entering the city of Rome. Note the white road width markings on the nearest vehicle and the stencil advising following drivers to keep back 30 meters. The unit emblem is painted in white as well.

An Opel Blitz of LAH traveling through Mediolan. The truck has a camouflage pattern of green and brown over the sand background. Sending LAH to Italy was a move calculated by Hitler to help draw the Fascists to the German cause. Italy formally surrendered on September 3, 1943.

The SS acquired a substantial amount of captured equipment in France in 1940, including this Chevrolet staff car completely covered in mud thrown up by the vehicle towing it, somewhere in Russia, October 1943. The driver is wearing an early style field service cap with the embroidered Totenkopf on the front and SS eagle on the side.

An Sd.Kfz.7 half-track modified for anti-aircraft duty by mounting a 2cm FlaK 38. This was quite unusual as vehicles this size usually mounted the heavier 2cm Flakvierling 38 or 3.7cm FlaK 36. It carries the license plate SS-273603 with the tactical sign for a towed anti-aircraft battery on the vehicle rear. An indistinguishable unit marking is painted on the opposite side. The shot was taken in October 1943 during anti-partisan action in the northern Ukraine.

SS officers question a civilian during anti-partisan actions behind the front in October 1943, while an SS-Oberscharführer and SS-Unterscharführer look on. The officer on the left is an SS-Obersturmführer from an unidentified SS unit while the officer on the right, an SS-Untersturmführer, is a member of the SD. The SD played an important role in anti-partisan warfare in Eastern Europe.

An MG34 machine gun crew emplacement protected with sand bags and a camouflage net. 7.SS-Freiwilligen-Gebirgs-Division "Prinz Eugen" was created for anti-partisan warfare and performed this duty almost until the end of the war. Though supplied with mostly obsolete equipment, it fought very well and often with brutality against its opponents.

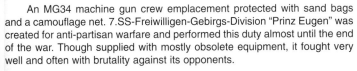

A patrol of 7.SS-Freiwilligen-Gebirgs-Division "Prinz Eugen" crossing a small stream in the mountains of Yugoslavia in 1943. Note the amount of personal equipment each man is forced to carry. They are carrying M31 rucksacks in olive green canvas which were very similar to civilian ones. This famous division was formed in March 1942 from ethnic German volunteers and conscripts from the Balkans and eastern European countries.

Soldiers from SS-Freiwilligen-Gebirgs-Artillerie-Regiment 7 talking with two Yugoslavian Muslim natives in 1943. The gun is a 7.5cm Gebirgsgeschütz 36 (Geb G36), a simple and reliable weapon that could be broken down into eight loads for transportation on pack animals. Note the "Odalrune" insignia on the collar patch of the soldier on the left.

SS and Croatian soldiers raise the German flag over a fortification occupied by the Italians prior to their capitulation in September 1943. The Ustashi and German troops fought hard in Yugoslavia and usually showed no mercy to Communist Partisans or civilians alike. Besides the 7.SS-Freiwilligen-Gebirgs-Division "Prinz Eugen", the 13.Waffen-Gebirgs-Division der SS "Handschar" (Kroatische Nr.1), 21.Waffen-Gebirgs-Division der SS "Skanderberg" (Albanische Nr.1) and 23.Waffen-Gebirgs-Division der SS "Kama" (Kroatische Nr.2) also fought in Yugoslavia.

Mountain troops also used donkeys as pack animals. Here, SS mountain troops cross a rocky stream. The soldier in the foreground, carrying an MG34 fitted with a drum magazine, wears the standard marching boots instead of the climbing boots normally issued to mountain troops.

The barrel of a 7.5cm Geb G36 being carried by a pack mule, the "prime mover" of the mountain troops. The mule is being led by an SS-Schütz wearing the new camouflage Feldmutze and a special "rucksack for artillery" for his personal belongings.

BP42 armored train Nr.64 used to support troops in anti-partisan actions in the Balkans 1943. The nearest wagon is armed with two 10.5cm gun turrets with a raised observation tower between them. The next wagon, the command one, is armed with a 2cm Flakvierling 38 anti-aircraft gun which could also be used against ground targets. The camouflage paint is quite visible on the nearest wagon, green and brown lines painted over the sand background. A white Totenkopf is painted on the side as well.

SS-Obergruppenführer "Sepp" Dietrich participates in a pistol fire exercise in November 1943. His medals and decorations include the Knights Cross with Oak Leaves and Swords, an honorary gold and diamond pilot/observer's badge on the center of the pocket with a round gold NSDAP badge and his WWI tank crewman's battle badge earned in 1918 and one of less than 100 awarded. On his left sleeve, above the SS eagle, is a Crimea battle shield. He was awarded the Diamonds to his Knights Cross on August 6, 1944 after 1 1/2 months of hard fighting against Montgomery's forces in the Caen area as commander of 1.SS-Panzer-Korps "Leibstandarte SS Adolf Hitler".

Winter 1943-44 in the Soviet Union saw no respite from battle for either side, which involved all available infantry and panzer divisions from the Wehrmacht and SS. Here a group of soldiers wearing the reversible two piece snow suit, white on one side with a camouflage print on the other, are taking a break from the action to have a meal. These uniforms lost their white appearance in a short time, but they were still more useful in the winter landscape than the inner camouflaged side. They also have the woolen toque and large mitts with separate trigger fingers worn over wool gloves. Each has a colored armband that utilized a color of the day to help identify friend from foe as the Soviets also wore similar winter suits. The tank visible in the background is a T-34/76.

41

Two SS soldiers in their bivouac during the winter of 1943-44. Both men are wearing the fur-lined anorak, which used the furs of many different animals, explaining the difference in color inside the hoods. Both have white painted helmets. Note the tent, made from various SS and Wehrmacht camouflage pattern Zeltbahn shelter quarters, which is even equipped with a stove.

An officer from 4.SS-Panzer-Grenadier-Division "Polizei" gives an order to open fire somewhere in the northern sector of the Eastern Front during the winter of 1943-44. He is wearing one of the earlier army style reversible suits with the field gray color on the outside. The Ordnungspolizei style collar insignia and Nazi shield on the right side of the helmet were typical for this SS division until February 1942 when they were integrated into the Waffen-SS and standard SS rank insignia was authorized to be worn.

A February 1944 winter day in the Southern Ukraine as the Germans are steadily being driven back by the Soviet Army. An SS-Unterscharführer with two men leads a pair of Bactrian camels, distinguished by their two humps, pulling carts filled with straw. The Germans had utilized camels for transport duties since the campaign in the Caucasus in 1942.

SS-Obersturmführer Hans Drexel of 2./SS-Panzer-Grenadier-Regiment "Westland" just after the battles around Cherkassy in March 1944. He was awarded the Knights Cross in the fall of 1943 and was later promoted to SS-Hauptsturmführer. He is wearing a sheepskin jacket over his uniform and appears to have his trousers tucked into his wool socks that have been rolled down over his lace up boots. Behind him is a Soviet ZIS-3 76.2mm anti-tank gun that has had a scruffy coat of white winter camouflage paint applied and is being towed by a half-track prime mover.

Soldiers of II.SS-Panzer-Korps retreating from the Tarnopol area around April 20, 1944. The nearest man is equipped with two M39 egg grenades and a pouch containing 18 cartridges for a flare gun. The second man in line, an SS-Scharführer, identifiable by the two stripes on the camouflage rank badge on his left sleeve, is wearing the new M44 camouflage drill uniform introduced in March that year. Farther back in line, one of the men carries an MG42 and others are carrying Panzerfausts. At the bottom of the hill, a Tiger from s.Pz.Abt.507 is mired in the mud.

An SS soldier, probably from 16.SS-Panzer-Grenadier-Division "Reichsführer-SS", on the front line somewhere in Italy in April 1944 is offered an orange by one of his comrades. He is wearing his standard SS uniform and has a Wehrmacht "Splinter" pattern camouflage helmet cover with loops for attaching foliage. He has also fixed a small bundle of straw under his shoulder strap. The man in the foreground is wearing an early style "Plane Tree" pattern smock.

Soldiers of II.SS-Panzer-Korps entering a town in the area of Tarnopol, where 9.SS-Panzer-Division "Hohenstaufen" and 10.SS-Panzer-Division "Frundsberg" fought their first battles in April 1944, opening a corridor to the surrounded 1.Panzer-Armee. The SS-Artillerie-Regiments were fully tracked and consisted of 12 Wespe with 10.5cm guns and 6 Hummel with 15cm guns plus two Hummel munitions carriers. Here we see a Wespe from the first battery with identification letter "F" painted on the front of the gunshield indicating the sixth gun in the battery. Note the letter is repeated on the muzzle brake cover. The two men walking on the left are wearing camouflage smocks over their greatcoats, a common practice often seen in these units.

After the battles around Tarnopol, II.SS-Panzer-Korps was withdrawn in May 1944, and put into action against partisans under the command of Heersgruppe Nord Ukraine. Here, two NCOs and another soldier were photographed during one of these operations in a small Ukrainian village.

A 8cm Granatwerfer 34 manned by SS troops in Italy, May 1944. These soldiers are wearing the Model 1942 type 1 camouflage smock identified by the pockets in the skirt and foliage loops sewn on to the shoulders and upper back. The smock on the man dropping the mortar bomb into the tube is a "Plane Tree" pattern and the other one is a "Blurred Edge" pattern. Note the camouflage face masks fixed to their helmets. The one in the foreground has an elasticized band.

In May 1944, about 600 men from SS-Fallschirmjäger-Bataillon 500 landed by glider and parachute at Drvar where Tito had his HQ at the time, narrowly missing capturing the partisan leader. Here we see two of them pulling a standard supply container with extra boxes of machine gun ammunition on it. These containers were dropped with the paratroops and carried additional weapons and ammunition along with other necessary supplies such as medical equipment and radios.

SS-Fallschirmjäger in a position on the outskirts of Drvar. They were trained by the Luftwaffe in a very short period of time and equipped the same as the Luftwaffe Fallschirmjäger units with helmets and camouflage smocks. They wore their standard SS uniforms under the smocks, but were otherwise identical in appearance.

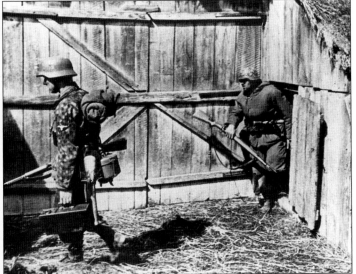

Two SS soldiers leaving a barn after searching it for partisans. The man on the left is wearing the new M44 camouflage drill uniform in the "Dot" pattern with the SS eagle on the left sleeve. All insignia were later eliminated although they continued to be worn throughout the rest of the war. The other man is wearing the two piece winter suit with the field gray side out.

This young SS soldier has flushed out a partisan or Red Army soldier from hiding, late May 1944. He is also wearing the new M44 camouflage drill uniform in the "Dot" pattern. The earliest versions of these uniforms were produced in autumn "Blurred Edge" or "Oak Leaf" patterns, though there are some instances of summer patterns being produced. Note the civilian blanket rolled up and carried on his back.

SS-Brigadeführer Jurgen Wagner, winner of the Knights Cross and commander of 23.SS-Freiwilligen-Panzer-Grenadier-Division "Nederland", talking to some of his young soldiers on the occasion of their decoration with the Iron Cross Second Class for bravery in combat, May 1944. Involved in anti-partisan operations in Croatia in the autumn of 1943, it was transferred to the Leningrad area in January 1944 and took part in the battles around Narva in the summer. All of them are wearing the M44 camouflage drill uniform except for the man standing at the back who wears the trousers only with his "Plane Tree" pattern smock and Wagner, who wears the tunic only. Helmet covers were not produced in the new pattern and so remained the same as before.

French civilians jostle each other for treats thrown by the SS crew of an Sd.Kfz.251/7 Ausf.D, the Pioniere version of this armored half-track, somewhere in France prior to the Allied invasion in Normandy. The vehicle is liberally covered in foliage as camouflage against roving Allied fighter bombers who had almost complete control of the air. The soldier leaning over the side of the vehicle is wearing a black panzer jacket with an army style piped Totenkopf collar patch and no evident cuffband. His M43 field gray Feldmutze has the SS eagle on the side on a black triangular patch.

An SS-Unterscharführer from SS-Panzer-Grenadier-Regiment 24 "Danmark" firing a flare pistol in the ruins of Libau in 1944. He has the Walther 27mm signal pistol and Mauser 98k rifle. This regiment was originally formed as "Freikorps Danmark". The name was changed to SS-Grenadier-Regiment 1 "Danmark" in July 1943. It fought in the Balkans and later, on the Eastern Front as part of 11.SS-Panzer-Grenadier-Division "Nordland" in the Narva area under SS-Brigadeführer Joachim Zeigler.

SS-Untersturmführer Michael Wittmann, most famous hero of the Waffen-SS during the battle of Normandy, shown here in a photo taken in mid-January 1944 after being awarded the Knights Cross. He was awarded the Oak Leaves two weeks later, which have been added rather poorly to this earlier photograph, and promoted. He joined the SS in 1937 and served in armored cars in Poland and France and StuG.III's in Greece and during the invasion of Russia. After SS officer training school, he was trained on the Tiger I in early 1943. He won his greatest fame for the almost single handed destruction of the British 22nd Armoured Brigade at the French town of Villers-Bocage on June 13, 1944 for which he was awarded the Swords to his Knights Cross and promoted again to SS-Hauptsturmführer. During his career, he claimed 138 tanks destroyed and 132 guns along with numerous other vehicles making him the highest scoring Panzer "Ace" of the war. He was killed, along with his crew, near St. Aignan-de-Cramesnil on August 8, 1944.

An old Schwerer Panzerspähwagen (Sd.Kfz.231) 8-Rad with the divisional emblem of 12.SS-Panzer-Division "Hitlerjugend" on the front moving through the demolished city of Caen in July 1944. The tactical number on the side of the turret has been painted over. The SS NCO riding on the side is wearing an M44 camouflage drill tunic in the "Dot" pattern over his field gray tunic, the collar of which is still visible, along with trousers made from Italian army camouflage material. Close to his left leg, a Panzerfaust "kleine" can be seen.

British POW's being led away guarded by two Waffen-SS NCOs, both wearing the M1936 field gray uniform with pleated pockets and M1943 field caps. The battle fought by 1.SS-Panzer-Korps "LSSAH" in Normandy against British, Canadian and Polish forces was, as Winston Churchill would say, "their finest hour". The heavy fighting caused many casualties among the SS troops due to total Allied ground and air superiority, but it would be difficult to find another example of such determined resistance in any other two month period of the war.

SS-Oberführer Fritz Kraemer, chief of staff of 1.SS-Panzer-Korps "Leibstandarte SS Adolf Hitler" in July 1944. Kraemer was a well educated Wehrmacht staff officer who joined the Waffen-SS in July 1943 as Dietrich's chief of staff. Without his excellent work, Dietrich, who was untrained for the position of a corps commander, would have had great difficulty in commanding a force of this size. He was promoted to SS-Brigadeführer and served as Dietrich's chief of staff of 6.Panzer-Armee from October 1944 until the end of the war. The young messenger in the foreground is wearing the M44 camouflage drill uniform in the "Dot" pattern.

Probably the most famous general in the German Army, Generalfeldmarshall Erwin Rommel is accompanied by SS-Obergruppenführer "Sepp" Dietrich in this photograph taken two days before his staff car was strafed by Allied fighters and he was wounded. Implicated in the July 20 attempt on Hitler's life, Rommel was forced to commit suicide on October 14 to avoid a public spectacle and protect his family, and given a state funeral.

An Sd.Kfz.250/3 of an unidentified SS division somewhere in France, August 1944. The battles in France during the summer resulted in severe losses in many of the high quality Waffen-SS and Wehrmacht divisions, which could not be adequately replaced. Nevertheless, they fought with tenacity in Hungary and on the Oder River and even during the Ardennes Offensive, showed some of the offensive fighting spirit with which they had become famous for.

Members of an SS unit man defensive positions somewhere in Central Europe. The soldier on the left is wearing a Model 1942 style camouflage smock in a "Plane Tree" pattern with an army "Splinter" pattern helmet cover with foliage loops.

SS troops remove fallen trees from the road to open the way for an Sd.Kfz.251/7 Ausf.C, the Pioniere version of this APC. Judging by the relatively new condition of this vehicle, this photo was probably taken in 1943. Partisan groups continually staged such actions to make life for the German soldiers as difficult as

A similar situation only a year later. Here SS troops are filling a ditch dug in the road overnight by the Polish underground movement in August 1944. In the background is another Pioniere APC, this one is an Sd.Kfz.251/7 Ausf.D which was first produced in September 1943. It is painted in a two color camouflage scheme with the barely visible tactical sign of an armored reconnaissance battalion painted on the upper left side of the front plate. Also visible is the license plate "SS-900008".

SS-Obersturmführer Karl Nicolessi-Leck, commander of 8./SS-Panzerregiment 5, second from the left between the Panther Ausf.A and the Sd.Kfz.251/3 Ausf.D, near Warsaw, August 1944. He was awarded the Knights Cross for action during the battle for Kovel when, on March 30, he broke through to the encircled city with seven Panthers and about 50 infantry. Between August 18-22, IV.SS-Panzer-Korps claimed 98 Soviet tanks destroyed in the battles around Warsaw.

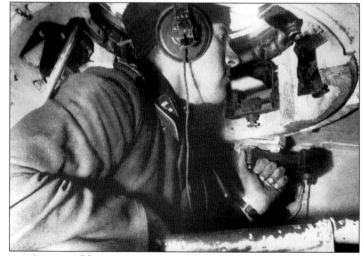

A young SS panzer commander views the battlefield through the periscopes in the cupola of his Panther. The Panther made its battle debut during "Operation Zitadelle" and suffered many losses due to mechanical failure. Later improvements made the Panther arguably the best tank in WWII.

SS-Sturmbannführer Erwin Meierdress, commander of 1./SS-Panzerregiment 3 of 3.SS-Panzer-Division "Totenkopf" who took part in the battles east of Warsaw, where his unit destroyed many Soviet tanks and SPGs. He was awarded the Oak Leaves to his Knights Cross on October 12, 1943, for his part in the battles in the southern Soviet Union, where he was wounded for the fifth time. He was killed in Hungary on January 4, 1945. The SS-Hauptsturmführer on the left is wearing the M44 camouflage drill uniform in the "Dot" pattern. Behind them is a knocked out T-34/85.

Two SS soldiers passing yet another T-34/85 destroyed in the battle. The man nearest the camera is wearing the M44 camouflage drill uniform in the "Dot" pattern while the other wears his field gray uniform. Each man carries only his weapon and ammunition.

A young SS-Sturmann of 3.SS-Panzer-Division "Totenkopf" waiting for the enemy on the outskirts of Warsaw in August 1944. He is wearing the M1943 tunic with the field gray collar and simplified pockets combined with trousers from the M44 camouflage drill uniform in the "Dot" pattern. His cuffband is one of the earlier type with the "Totenkopf" emblem. Cuffbands with the division name in block letters replaced them in 1943 although they continued to be worn.

More SS soldiers of IV.SS-Panzer-Korps which fought against units of the Soviet 2nd Tank Army in the fields east of Warsaw in August 1944, racing past a burning T-34/85.

An example of a combat vehicle rarely seen on the battlefield in the summer of 1944 is this Schwerer Panzerspähwagen (Sd.Kfz.231) 6-Rad. Originally in service with an SS police unit, it was captured by Polish partisans on August 26, 1944, in the Kurow area. It had been repainted in an overall sand color and carried the national cross and a tactical marking painted on the side. The soldier in the turret appears to be wearing a captured German uniform complete with helmet and stick grenade in his belt.

Heinrich Himmler inspects young volunteers into the Waffen-SS from the quasi-military Hitler Youth movement. Reserves in the Third Reich in the autumn of 1944 were very limited and the Waffen-SS, as well as the Wehrmacht, were forced to accept young boys and old men into their ranks. The Hitler Youth were fanatical and ready to sacrifice but their lack of training and experience resulted in unnecessarily high losses.

The last day of the war in Berlin, May 1945. SS troops work under Soviet direction to extinguish the fire in a burning SS truck. Many SS troops followed orders to fight to the last bullet and preferred an honorable death on the battlefield than to surrender and ended in the POW camps in the Soviet Union. Many also chose to flee to the west to surrender to the Allied armies. Regardless of the choice, many of the hardest core SS members lost their lives in the last two weeks of the war and during the following years of captivity in Soviet and Allied prison camps.